Cont

Introduction

A
STRAIGHTFORWARD
GUIDE
TO
BUYING AND SELLING
PROPERTY AT AUCTION

ROGER SPROSTON BA MSc

Straightforward Publishing

30108   036338395

Straightforward Guides

© Straightforward Co Ltd 2025

978-1-80236-400-2

Printed by 4edge www.4edge.co.uk

Cover design by BW Studio Derby

Publisher: Straightforward Publishing, Derby, United Kingdom
EU Authorised Representative: Easy Access System Europe-Mustamae tee 50 10621 Tallin, Estonia, *gpsr.requests@easproject.com*

Whilst every effort has been made to ensure that the information contained within this book is correct at the time of going to press, the author and publisher can take no responsibility for the errors or omissions contained within.

****

Introduction

Most of us have watched programmes on television such as 'Homes Under the Hammer'. This involves people, mainly investors, purchasing a property at auction, refurbishing it selling it on or renting it out. However, there are also many non-investors looking to buy a property at a decent price and live in it as their main home. This book, updated to **2025**, is intended for both investors and would be home buyers. It is also intended for those who wish to sell at auction and covers the large variety of other properties that come up for auction, including commercial properties.

At the time of writing, the property market is overheated, with prices out of control, particularly in the south of the country and rents everywhere off the scale. In short, the market is in a mess and works against the consumer and also a stable society. A correction is long overdue. This is why people are increasingly going to auction to secure a bargain.

Auctions generally

In addition to providing advice and information for buyers of property, the book also offers advice for the seller, explaining how the auction process works.

For those buying a residential property at auction, auctions can mean that buying a house doesn't involve endless viewings with estate agents and then months of waiting to exchange contracts, with the possibility of gazumping along the way. Once you have made your bid and the gavel comes down then the property is yours on the spot.

Buying a house, particularly in the distorted London housing market, can now be an extremely frustrating and uncertain process. This is why buyers are now looking to auctions to circumvent the hassle of looking for, or selling, a house.

With house prices continuing to rise, people are looking for value, looking for some way to get onto the property ladder and are turning to auctions, where there are still bargains to be found and the usual rules relating to house purchase do not apply. Changes to stamp duty due to take place in April 2025 have also provided a surge in demand. Even after the stamp duty deadline, auctions will still remain a popular way to buy and sell.

Needless to say, there are many things to watch out for and many pitfalls to avoid when buying property at auction. These will be discussed in depth in this book. In short, when buying at auction:

- be certain of what you want and what you want to do with it.
- Never rely on the catalogue alone-always go to see the property.
- If possible, get a surveyor involved before making a bid for the property-this will save you a lot of time and money later.
- Talk to the auctioneer in advance of the sale-they are duty bound to let you know of any problems that they know of.
- Make sure that you understand the legal pack and have a firm idea of what you are letting yourself in for.
- Make sure that you have the finance in place.
- make sure that you understand the process-try to attend an auction before you put in your own bids.

This book should prove invaluable in taking you through the process of buying (and selling) property at auction and put you in a strong position when bidding. Remember, if buying, as we have stated above, when the gavel falls the property is yours-make sure that you have bought the right one and are on safe ground.

****

Chapter 1

How Auctions Work

Whilst most of us have a basic idea of how auctions work, and have watched various programmes which deal with property and other lots, it is important to delve a little deeper and gain a broad understanding of what an auction is, specifically a property auction, what can be bought and sold at property auctions and how we can close deals and get what we want on the day.

The below is a general overview of how an auction works and what actually happens on the day. It offers advice to both buyers and sellers. We will be discussing each area in detail in the following chapters. However, this will give you a general flavour of the whole process.

What is a property auction?

The process is very similar to the normal method of private sale. However, for an auction sale the seller and their solicitor carry out all the necessary paperwork and legal investigations prior to the auction. Subject to the property receiving an acceptable bid, the property will be 'sold' on auction day with a legally binding exchange of contracts and a fixed completion date.

Online property auctions

Auctions, and particularly online auctions, have become an increasingly popular way of buying and selling, especially in the past few years since Covid. This offers many advantages to both sellers and buyers. .

The rise of online auctions

Online property auctions have been offered for a number of years now. During COVID-19 restrictions, auctions couldn't take place in-person. Because of this, some auction houses quickly switched to online-only offerings. These kinds of auctions provide a unique and modern way to buy and sell. Since the end of restrictions, many auction houses have developed a hybrid structure moving forward, allowing buyers to make bids in-person and online.

14

Different types of property auction houses

Auction houses vary in size and the amount of business that they conduct and the frequency with which they hold auctions. Most will sell both residential and commercial property and each will have its own style of operation, and fee structure.

Large auction houses will hold auctions frequently, perhaps every two months and will have around 250 lots for sale. A lot of the auctions happen in London but will also be held nearer to home. Therefore, a large estate agent which has its main base in the Midlands, and also holds auctions, will tend to have them in Birmingham, Derby, and in the case of the auction we attended, featured in the final chapter, in Nottingham.

Most of the large auction houses will deal with property put forward by large institutions, such as banks selling repossessions and also local authorities and will advertise the sales in the mainstream media and trade papers. The medium size auction houses will hold auctions as frequently as they can, in regional venues, such as racecourses and conference centres, and depending on stock, usually every two to three months, tending to advertise locally. The small auction houses will have far fewer lots and will hold their sales in smaller local venues.

They may advertise in local press but more often will trade on word of mouth.

Those who attend auctions

As you might imagine, all sorts of people attend auctions. The common denominator is that they are all interested in buying property.

Property investors are most common at auction, people who are gradually building a portfolio or those who have large portfolios that they wish to expand. They tend to fall into two groups, those who are after capital appreciation, i.e. buy at a low value and build the capital value and those who are looking for rental income. Then there are the property traders who like a quick profit from buying and 'flipping' property. These types usually have intimate knowledge of an area and are well placed to make a quick profit.

Then we have the developers who look for small profitable sites or larger sites where property can be built and sold on. The sites can have existing buildings on them or can be vacant lots with or without planning permission. Last, but not least, we have those people who intend to buy solely for the purpose of owner occupation, look to buy a below-value property that they can redesign and make their own.

What types of property are suitable for auction?

There is strong demand for all types of properties offered at auction. These may be properties requiring updating, those with short leases, development sites with or without planning permission, repossessions, forced sales, investment properties, ground rents, probates, receivership sales and local authority properties. However, any type of property can be sold at auction and initially the property will be inspected to discuss specific criteria and the current situation. Extensive research will be carried out by the auction house and advice offered as to whether auction is the appropriate method of sale.

The below represents a cross section of what might be found at auction.

Properties for Improvement

Properties in need of updating make ideal auction Lots. They are in great demand from refurbishment specialists and private buyers, keen to undertake a project for their own occupation or for resale. They also appeal to buy-to-let investors who carry out the improvements then retain them as part of a property portfolio.

Tenanted Properties

Residential houses and flats with tenants in residence sell well at auction. Notice doesn't need to be served notice on tenants, and rental income continues to be received right up to completion.

Residential Investments

Houses in multiple occupation and blocks of flats are sold at auction as valuable investments. Here it is the rent level that determines the sale price, just as much as the building itself.

Development Propositions

Derelict or disused farm buildings, empty commercial premises, buildings with potential for conversion or change of use, can all sell well at auction. In some locations a change to residential can significantly add to the value of a property, in other situations there may be space for additional dwellings or to substantially enlarge the property.

Development propositions and planning permission

Planning permission is granted by the local authority for extensive changes to property. Never begin any renovation or alterations to a property without first checking with your local authority.

Location is an important factor so if your property lies in an area of outstanding natural beauty there may be more restrictions on what can be done. Small renovations like changing windows and doors, changing bathrooms or kitchens and building a porch do not usually require planning permission but you should always check.

This is particularly true for unusual properties and listed buildings.

For extensive renovations planning permission is usually required.

If you are buying a renovation property at auction and it already has planning permission, be sure to check the expiry date. Planning permission can run for three years but an extension may be allowed if the work is underway.

Building Land

There is no better way of ensuring a seller achieves best price for a building plot or parcel of development land than to offer it for sale by auction. Builders will be able to consult with architects, planners etc., and be ready to bid in the auction room.

Mixed Use Properties

Properties that have twin uses or a variety of potential future uses are ideal for sale by auction. Retail shops with accommodation above appeal to investors as well as owner-occupiers. Further conversion work can often be undertaken and the property tailored to suit the purchaser's special requirements.

Commercial Investments

Retail shops, offices, industrial units, garage blocks and parking areas - an ever increasing number of commercial investments are being sold at auction. It doesn't matter whether they are vacant or tenanted, with lease renewal soon needed or with a long way to run.

Unique Properties

There are always some rare entries, sought after property and prime locations that need to be sold in a competitive bidding environment. Unexpectedly high prices have been achieved by this route.

Amenity Land and Other Property

Paddocks, meadows, fields, moorings, amenity land and also other unusual land parcels are all sold at auction. If it is property or land that is surplus to requirements, the likelihood is a buyer can be found at auction. If it has a value, and is worth marketing, it is worth considering a disposal by auction.

What is the timeframe for an auction sale?

The latest date for entering property for an auction is usually five to six weeks prior to the auction. Once the marketing agreement has been signed, the property will be placed in the catalogue and a board erected. Each seller's legal representative will be contacted to obtain a legal pack, which the seller must produce. This pack should generally include office copy entries and plans, the local search, leases (if applicable) and any other relevant documents. All properties at auction are sold under the General Conditions of Sale and, with the legal pack, also require any Special Conditions of Sale to be attached. These are matters that are relevant solely to the lot being sold. The marketing period starts five to six weeks before a sale. The details of all the lots to be offered in the next sale, including colour photographs of each property, viewing arrangements and any other relevant information will then be published. A few days prior to the auction, the reserve price will be agreed.

What happens on the day?

The lots will be offered and the bidding taken to the highest possible level and once the gavel falls, the contracts will be exchanged. The buyer purchases the property at the price they bid - this cannot be negotiated and the stipulated terms cannot be changed. The buyer will then pay 10% of the purchase price on the day and completion occur 28 days later. The funds are then paid to the seller less the fees of the Auctioneers and those of the seller's solicitor.

The atmosphere of an auction room can be extremely exciting and competitive and it is often the case that an interested party will bid in excess of the figure that had previously been set as their maximum. In some cases, the prices achieved at auction can be higher than those achieved by private treaty.

Now read the main points from chapter 1 overleaf.

****

Main points from chapter 1

- An auction sale facilitates the quick sale of a property, with sale and completion often taking place within one month of the successful bid.
- All sorts of property is suitable for auction and there are a variety of reasons for selling properties.
- Auction houses vary in size and the amount of business that they conduct and the frequency with which they hold auctions. Most will sell both residential and commercial property and each will have its own style of operation, and fee structure.
- All sorts of people attend auction, from investors to institutions to potential owner occupiers. The common denominator is that they are all interested in buying property.

****

Chapter 2

Selling at Auction

Advantages of selling at an auction

An auction is an efficient and cost-effective way of selling property and if prepared properly with intensive marketing, advertising and mailing, will result in the greatest possible exposure of the lots offered.

To maximize the effectiveness of the marketing, considerable thought must be given to the guide price, which needs to be tailored to generate competitive bidding in the auction room, thus ensuring that the best price is being achieved. Although some properties are more suitable for sale by private treaty, taking this route does present uncertainties over terms such as sale price and timing of exchange and completion.

Selling by auction, however, offers a high degree of certainty that a sale will be achieved on a given day and, significantly, on the fall of the gavel an immediate binding contract is formed. As no further negotiation is permitted the entire sale process, from instruction to exchange of contracts can be achieved within as little as four weeks.

For vendors with a large number of properties to sell, auctions provide a highly efficient method of sale allowing for a total or phased disposal programme selling in individual lots thus maximising receipts. For those selling in a fiduciary capacity, there is the added advantage of the sale being entirely open and transparent.

Most types of property are suitable for auction provided that a realistic reserve price is agreed.

Who sells at auction?

Auction is now regarded as the optimum method of sale for many sellers who range from private investors and property companies to banks, housing associations and local authorities.

When do you want to sell?

Decide when you want to sell your property and which auction you would like to put it in. Sale dates and venues can be found on auctioneer's websites.

What information do auctioneers need?

In order to give you the best possible advice auctioneers will need the following details:

- Address
- Description
- Photograph
- Tenure and Tenancy (if applicable) details
- Floor plan or site plan
- Anything else you consider to be material

Once the auctioneers have received this information, they will provide an estimate of the likely sale price of your property at Auction. Together with a proposed reserve, they will send you a copy of their standard agency contract setting out their terms and conditions. Once the maximum reserve price is agreed you will be asked to sign and return the standard agency contract to confirm your instructions, at which time the Entry Fee becomes payable.

Proof of identity-If an auctioneer has not sold for you before they will require proof of your identity and address before they can market your property.

How much does it cost to sell?

All auctioneers will charge a fee to enter a property into an auction. This fee is payable whether the property is sold or not. The fee is a contribution towards the cost of marketing and catalogue production. The fee will depend on how much space is taken in the catalogue for the property.

Commission

In the event of a sale, an auctioneer's commission is up to 2.5% of the sale price plus VAT for a sole agency or 3.% plus VAT for a joint agency. A joint agency is usually advisable where the auctioneer feels it is necessary to include a local estate agent to handle local enquiries and conduct viewings. The auction house surveyors will confirm the auction entry fee and commission rate with you in writing before accepting your instructions.

Sales particulars

Once the auctioneer has been formally instructed, the property will be inspected by one of their surveyors, measurements taken where appropriate, and the property will be photographed. Draft sales particulars will then be forwarded to you and to your solicitors for approval and/or amendments.

Legal documents

At the same time your solicitors will be instructed to prepare a legal pack containing special conditions of sale, title documents, leases (where applicable), searches, planning documentation and office copy entries so that they are available to interested parties either by post or online.

Guide price

The auction team will recommend a guide price which you will need to approve before marketing begins. It is important to set the guide price at a realistic level which is attractive to buyers. This will generate competitive bidding in the auction room and ensure that best value is achieved.

Marketing your property

Marketing will usually start approximately three to four weeks prior to the auction sale. Auction Houses produce thousands of catalogues for each auction. These are sent to prospective buyers such as private investors, property companies and developers.

E-marketing

Catalogues are available online and auctioneers send regular email alerts to the private investors who are registered on the site.

Advertising and PR

Good auctioneers will advertise in the key property publications and place advertisements in local newspapers.

Targeted Marketing

Auction houses also target individuals who have previously expressed an interest in similar properties, as well as adjacent occupiers, local agents, local developers, builders and property companies.

Viewings and Surveys

Potential purchasers may want to view your property during the marketing period and have a survey carried out. You should let the auctioneer know how you would prefer viewings to be arranged and we shall arrange access for buyers. In most cases, vacant properties are open at prearranged times for viewing. Details will be printed in the catalogue.

Legal documentation

In conjunction with your solicitors the auction house will supply copy documents to prospective purchaser's solicitors and will keep you constantly updated as to the levels of interest shown.

The reserve price

The auction House will agree a reserve price with you for your property a few days before the auction. This is the level below which they will not be authorised to sell. It is important that this be set at a realistic level.

Auction day-the fall of the gavel

On the fall of the Auctioneer's gavel, a binding contract is effected. The successful bidder is required to provide the name, address and telephone number of the purchaser and the purchaser's solicitors. The successful bidder will also be asked to provide a deposit for 10% of the purchase price. Identification of the purchaser is always checked at this stage.

Clearance of all deposit cheques is arranged immediately after the auction.

Exchange of Contracts

The Memorandum of Sale is made up in the room and given to the purchaser to sign. The exchange is overseen by the auction house's solicitor. They will forward the purchaser's signed Memorandum of Sale to your solicitor. Completion will usually, take place 20 working days later. The deposit funds are then paid to you less fees.

What happens if the property does not sell on the day?

If your property fails to reach its reserve in the room, someone may still wish to buy it. You will need to decide whether to accept any offer and advise the auction house accordingly. The property may even be sold in the days or weeks after the sale as most auction houses continue to market the property.

Now read the Main Points from Chapter 2 overleaf.

****

Main points from chapter 2

- An auction is an efficient and cost-effective way of selling property and if prepared properly with intensive marketing, advertising and mailing, will result in the greatest possible exposure of the lots offered.

- To maximize the effectiveness of the marketing, considerable thought must be given to the guide price, which needs to be tailored to generate competitive bidding in the auction room, thus ensuring that the best price is being achieved.

- All auctioneers will charge a fee to enter a property into an auction. This fee is payable whether the property is sold or not.

- On the fall of the Auctioneer's gavel, a binding contract is effected. The successful bidder is required to provide the name, address and telephone number of the purchaser and the purchaser's solicitors. The successful bidder will also be asked to provide a deposit for 10% of the purchase price. Identification of the purchaser is always checked at this stage. Clearance of all deposit cheques is arranged immediately after the auction.

****

Chapter 3

Buying Property at Auction

We have seen how properties are sold at auction. It is significantly easier to sell than to buy property at auction, because of all the background work that is needed before deciding to bid. Of course, this depends on what you want to do with a property once you have bought it. The following chapters deal with the process of bidding for a property and everything that underpins this. This chapter deals with the general process at auction.

How and why do I buy at auction?

Buying at auction is an assured way of securing a purchase. Once a bid is accepted, contracts will be exchanged on the day of the sale. The seller cannot withdraw from the sale, nor is it possible for any kind of gazumping to take place. Due to auctions being conducted in public, there can be no secret bidding or unfair competition and once the gavel comes down, the successful bidder is legally committed to pay the agreed price and complete the purchase. Another attraction of buying at auction is that properties are usually offered at a realistic guide price, particularly when in need of repair, refurbishment or being sold by a financial organisation to recover debts.

Why is property being sold at an auction?

There are a number of reasons why property is sold at an auction:

- A quick sale is needed, often due to the owner being in financial difficulties or it is a repossession
- There are structural problems that prevent the property being sold easily in the conventional manner.
- Properties sold by public bodies. Here you get all sort of property, including weird and wonderful properties such as public toilets and police stations, all of which may have their uses.

❑ The property is unique and there are no direct comparisons, such as lighthouses and the above-mentioned public toilet.

It is always best to find out why exactly the property is being sold at auction. Is it so difficult to get rid of because of some inherent reason? Ask why is this property at auction and not being sold in the conventional way. Who exactly is the vendor and what if any are the problems stopping it being sold conventionally? The reasons that the property is at auction may be entirely innocent but it is always worth finding out to avoid future problems.

The seller will provide a legal pack that may be inspected at any time. Auctioneers will strongly advise that professional advice is obtained from a legal representative. Details of the seller's solicitors will be available and, should a mortgage be required, it is available to have this in place prior to the sale. Again, Auctioneers strongly advise that funding is discussed with a professional advisor prior to attending the sale.

The successful buyer will be required to pay 10% of the purchase price on the day, together with a buyer's premium which is normally around £250 including VAT, although this should be checked. The balance of the purchase price is required on the agreed completion day and this is normally 28 days after the auction, however this can vary so best to check with the auction house.

What happens next?

Once you have found your auction, to receive a complimentary auction catalogue you should contact the Auctioneers and this will give the information about the properties being offered for sale. You can also download a catalogue from the auctioneer's website. The catalogue includes descriptions of the available properties, legal information, viewing arrangements and a guide price, which is purely an indication of a realistic selling price. This should not be taken as a firm asking or selling price and should be relied upon as a guide only.

Professional advice must be taken in relation to any lot in which there is an interest.

For lots where viewings are arranged, these are carried out on a block basis and are published in all advertising and in the auction catalogue. Any prospective purchaser is welcome at these viewings and should the scheduled appointments be inconvenient, alternative arrangements can be made. Any interest must be registered with the auctioneers in order that prospective purchasers may be kept informed as to the progress of the sale.

How do prospective purchasers find out legal and survey information?

A legal pack is requested from each of the vendor's solicitors and this contains copies of all legal papers, which will be required by any prospective purchasers for them to make an informed decision regarding the purchase of any lot. The pack will include office copy entries and plans, the relevant local authority search, leases (if applicable), Special Conditions of Sale, replies to pre-contract enquiries and any other relevant documents. A copy of these legal packs can usually be obtained from auctioneers for a small charge. Should any additional information be required, the seller's solicitors are listed in the catalogue and can be contacted directly. All legal packs are available for inspection at each auction-any purchase at auction takes place under the assumption that all documentation and the terms of the contract have been read. It is strongly recommended that any potential purchasers carry out full investigations for any lot in which they have an interest and a survey is an integral part of that investigation.

How is finance arranged?

Should a mortgage be required, approval in principle must be obtained prior to auction. Lenders are familiar with the auction process and are usually willing to provide a mortgage offer for buyers intending to purchase at auction. A valuation and survey will be required along with legal evidence that there are no issues that will affect the value.

It is essential that the lender can provide funds within the timescale for completion. On the day of the auction, the purchaser will need to pay 10% of the purchase price and must ensure there are cleared funds to pay this amount. Sometimes, finance can be arranged through an Auctioneers on request.

Can lots be bought before auction?

Vendors may consider offers submitted before auction day. Any such offers need to be submitted in writing to an Auctioneers - this will be referred to the vendor and their instruction will be passed on to the prospective purchaser. Any offers will have to be unconditional and the buyer must be in a position to exchange contracts and pay the required deposit before auction day. With most auctioneers, no offers are considered within five days of the auction.

What happens on auction day?

Buyers should check on the day before the auction that any required lots are still available. Early arrival at the auction is recommended to ensure the Auctioneer's announcements are noted regarding withdrawn lots and changes in the order of the sale. The Auctioneer will make pre-auction announcements regarding the conduct at auction. Knowledge of these is strongly recommended. The Auctioneer will start the bidding by invitation and bids can be made by raising either a hand or the catalogue. In most cases an auction number will be issued prior to the bidding which will identify your bid.

All bidders in the room, including those online, will have an equal opportunity to bid and the auction team will be available for support. Once the desired price is reached, the Auctioneer will announce that the gavel is about to fall and the property will be deemed sold. The successful buyer will be the person with the highest bid at the time the gavel falls. Contracts are then exchanged and the successful purchaser will be invited to the legal desk to pay the 10% deposit, the buyers fee and to sign the sales memorandum.

What should I take with me to the auction room?

The items required are as follows:

- Deposit cheque or banker's draft for any potential purchase
- Identification - this is legally required under the money laundering regulations. Therefore, a driving licence or passport is required and a current utility bill to show proof of residence.
- Details of solicitors acting on behalf of any potential purchaser.

Prospective purchaser is unable to attend the auction?

If prospective purchasers are unable to attend the sale, it is possible to bid in other ways:

- By telephone - the interested party will be telephoned as the lot is being auctioned.
- Online bidding
- By proxy in writing - a member of the auction team will represent the buyer, who has previously specified their maximum bid
- Bid from your smartphone (see overleaf)

In each case a registration form and cheque to cover the deposit and buyer's fee, are required prior to the date of the auction. A bidder's registration form is printed in the catalogue or alternatively can be obtained from the office.

Bidding from your smartphone

A new e'Bay for homebuyers' is already big business making it easy to bid and buy via smartphone. Homeowners who are wary of the auction room when it comes to buying or selling might prefer a new digital online auction called BidX1 (bidx1.com). It is a bit like online goods market eBay but for property – and the latest sale is today.

Difficulties of raising finance, bargains that turn into bottomless pits, fears about losing deposits, overbidding, and auctioneers plucking "2 bids off the wall" still put many off the traditional "ballroom" auction. But BidX1, up and running in the UK for several years now, could be modifying that image.

Most significant is the holding of a £4,500 "buyers fee" at registration to enable you to bid. If you win with the highest bid, you must pay a 10 per cent deposit at once and complete the purchase in 20 business days, possibly extended if it is over Christmas. Each time the highest bid is made, the auction automatically extends for a further minute and only closes when there are no further bids.

BidX1's registration system for buyers and sellers complies with UK money laundering regulations and enables both sides to see on-screen who is bidding, how much, and when. BidX1's system can also see where the bid is from geographically and on what sort of device it was made.

Customers can view, bid, buy and sell from home on a mobile phone. And it seems the detailed knowledge and visibility of who is bidding and what is of interest to both residential and commercial buyers and sellers is transparent because records can be checked. BidX1's fees are one-and-a- half to two-and-a half per-cent of the sale price, depending on the sale and complexity of what's offered.

Will the property be insured when I purchase?

No - the purchaser at auction is responsible for obtaining Building insurance cover from the moment the property is deemed sold to them at auction.

Now read the main points from chapter 3 overleaf.

****

Main points from chapter 3

- Buying at auction is an assured way of securing a purchase. Once a bid is accepted, contracts will be exchanged on the day of the sale. The seller cannot withdraw from the sale, nor is it possible for any kind of gazumping to take place.

- Due to auctions being conducted in public, there can be no secret bidding or unfair competition and once the gavel comes down, the successful bidder is legally committed to both pay the agreed price and complete the purchase.

- It is always best to find out why exactly the property is being sold at auction. Is it so difficult to get rid of because of some inherent reason? Ask why is this property at auction and not being sold in the conventional way? Who exactly is the vendor and what if any are the problems stopping it being sold conventionally?

- Once you have found your auction, to receive a complimentary auction catalogue you should contact the Auctioneers and this will give the information about the properties being offered for sale. You can also download a catalogue from the auctioneer's website.

- Buyers should check the day before the auction that any required lots are still available. Early arrival at the auction is recommended to ensure the Auctioneer's announcement are noted regarding withdrawn lots and changes in the order of the sale.

****

Chapter 4

How to Go About Finding a Property at Auction

There are many property auctions being held all over the UK every day, including online auctions. Where you choose to buy at auction very much depends on what you want to buy, what is the intended use for the property, residential investment, commercial investment or a property for your own home.

Most people tend to concentrate on the area that they know. However, a few adventurous souls will branch out further afield. In order to find out the whereabouts of property auctions you will want to get hold of one of the main publications such as *Property Investor News* which is a magazine devoted entirely to property auctions in the UK.

You will have to pay for this magazine by subscription, details of which can be found at http://www.property-investor-news.com/auctions.html.

The organ of the surveying world, The Estates Gazette, which is a weekly publication also features some property auctions.

One other invaluable source of information is the Essential Information Group:

https://www.eigpropertyauctions.co.uk This is the news source for serious investors at auction. It is subscription based.

The Essential Information Group was formed in 1990 to provide the property industry with detailed information as to the results of all London property auctions. It now covers the whole of the UK and is recognised as the industry standard for auction information and currently includes details on over 500,000 properties and over 35,000 lots each year worth in excess of £5.5 billion. A range of services are available and they work closely with over 450 different auction houses arranging the transmission of guide prices, results and the provision of catalogues for interested parties. They also host a variety of Premium Rate services including a LiveLink service where people can listen live to an auction via telephone, thus allowing as many people as possible to access these auction details. The EIG have close ties with many auction houses where they provide services for viewing live property auctions on the internet. You can check out their online auctions page to see what auctions are going to be broadcast live. For more information on the Essential Information Group you should contact the address and website below.

By Post	By Phone	By Email
Essential Information Group Chapter House 33 London Road Reigate Surrey RH2 9HZ	01737 226150	Account Enquiries: accounts@eigroup.co.uk Sales and subscription enquiries: sales@eigroup.co.uk

Once you have found the auction houses(s) that you want to deal with you can go on their mailing list. There is a list of auction houses in the appendix with contact details. There are a number of websites which provide free auction lists, such as www.propertyauctionaction.co.uk. You can also often find auction catalogues online at the auction house website.

Repossessions

Increasing problems in the housing market and an increase in repossessions have led to more buyers turning to auction houses. But while you may be able to pick up a discount, there are risks involved.

For people interested in buying, seeking out a repossessed home represents a real opportunity to snap up a property at a discount. However, you need to know where to look - and also consider the risks involved, especially if you are planning to buy through an auction.

Where to find repossessed property

The repossession process is fairly complicated, and begins when a homeowner gets into difficulties meeting their monthly repayments

After a lender has taken possession of a property, it is likely to appoint an asset manager to ensure it is empty, clean and ready to sell. The property will then either be put on the market through an estate agent or sold directly through an auction. The method of selling the property will depend on its value in the market; if the lender is looking for a quick sale, it may opt for an auction. However, if it feels the property is likely to attract a lot of attention, it may decide an estate agent is the best way to achieve a sale.

The Essential Information Group provides information on chain-free properties, including repossessed flats and houses, probate homes and unsold new homes from property developers.

The website allows you to search for property by price, postcode or description; when you find one you like, you simply contact the estate agent involved. The one thing every home has in common is that there is no chain involved.

Auctions, meanwhile, might be more useful because the process can be a lot quicker – once the hammer falls the lot is technically yours and the sale then must complete within 28 days.

Another advantage of buying at auction is that you can usually get a good deal – while there are no exact figures on this, experts generally say buyers can save up to 30%. However, the actual price you achieve will depend on the type of property, why it is being sold at auction and how many people are interested – a lot of competition could drive up the price.

Perusing the auctioneer's catalogue

An auction house will release their catalogue several weeks before the auction begins. The catalogue will be in hard copy form or electronic form. This doesn't give much time for the prospective purchaser to look at what is on offer and arrange a viewing and get everything else in order. However, that is the nature of auctions. Quick processes and quick disposals.

Below is an extract from an auctioneer's catalogue (www.eddisons.com). This is an online catalogue, (dated several years ago), so there will be references to 'click here' for further information.

Lot No:203 Guide Price (£): 115,000 - 120,000*

Viewing Details

Date	Time
2nd Sep 20	14:00
9th Sep 20	14:00
17th Sep 20	14:00

The former Halton Wine and Food Store, 21-23 Chapel street, Halton, Leeds, LS15 7RN.

Status: Available

Category: Vacant Commercial

Venue (Auction)

Auction date: 18th September 20

Instructed by: The Joint LPA Receivers

Details: vacant corner retail premises with spacious 4 bedroom residential accommodation over two floors-workshop and yard providing off street parking.

Location. the property occupies a prominent position on Chapel Street in close proximity to the main shopping parade in Halton Leeds.

Ground Floor: retail Sales Area-extending to 49.79m2 (536ft2)

Residential accommodation-Lounge dining area kitchen WC

First floor-Four bedrooms (one with shower) bathroom WC

Outside-Secure gated yard providing parking for cars. Brick built garage/workshop

Note: All measurements are approximate and taken by a third party.

The above extract which although from an auction now gone, is typical of an auctioneer's catalogue and provides enough detail for a prospective bidder to make up their mind to view. It is always very advisable indeed to view the property in question. Some don't and live to regret what they have bought. By viewing you can get an idea of what you are entering into and what you might need to spend bringing the property back into a condition where you can rent or sell (or live in).

The catalogue starts with the lot number and then a photo, usually one photo but sometimes more. the viewing dates are listed along with the address and the status, i.e. available, along with the category, in this case vacant commercial. The venue of the auction is mentioned and the date, along with who instructed the property to auction.

Then the catalogue will provide property details and location followed by more detail as to the property size and numbers of rooms, parking etc. The information in the catalogue should provide sufficient detail to enable the prospective purchaser to go to the next stage and view the property then attend the auction.

The order of lots in the catalogue

An auction catalogue consists of Lots, and they will be numbered in the order at which they will be sold at auction. It is the practice of some auction houses to put the most popular lot at the start of the auction to draw bidders in. They will also intersperse less popular lots with the popular lots to ensure that bidder levels are maintained and people don't drift away after the 'sexy' lots have sold. It is important to remember that auction houses want to create an atmosphere of excitement on the day so that people will bid for what is on offer.

Although people can bid by phone or online for a lot, still the most popular method is to attend the auction room.

The guide price

The guide prices for properties at auction will vary, depending on what is for sale and where it is. Market forces will dictate this, as they do for property sold in the conventional way. However, for a good many properties the price will be set low, which reflects the condition of the property and also reflects the fact that the auctioneer wants to draw people in to bidding. In many cases, auctioneers will drop the guide price at the outset as most people won't start bidding at the actual starting price.

Therefore, you will find that if a house is valued at £160,000 the auctioneer will open with this then drop down to £150,000 to start the bidding. Guide prices are dictated by the reserve price on the lot. Sellers will have a price that they will not go under. This price is not disclosed to potential bidders before the auction but will affect the price at which the auctioneer starts the process. So, if a property is £160,000 and the auctioneer starts at £150,000 then £150,000 will be at the reserve price or just above.

Finding a property suitable for you in an auction catalogue

Once you have either been sent, or downloaded, a catalogue then you will need to identify the property or properties that you want to view and are interested in bidding for. There is quite a lot of background work to do before the auction begins. You will usually have about two weeks to start the ball rolling. After having identified a property suitable for you, you will need to arrange a viewing.

Viewing an auction property

As we have seen above with the auctioneers' particulars, viewing times are usually set by the auction and shown in their catalogue and you will have to fit in with these times. They are very much like estate agents block bookings. The number of viewings is limited and you will usually get the opportunity to view three or four times before auction. The people who show the property will not usually have any idea about the details of the property, being employed as key holders to show interested parties around. They will take details of all those who have viewed. The viewings are in half-hour slots. Although the viewing times are stated in the catalogue it is always best to play safe and confirm the times as they can change. If you have travelled a long way to attend a viewing only to find out it has been cancelled or rescheduled this can be very annoying, to say the least.

You will need to get used to the fact that if a property is popular and attracting lots of interest then there may be lots of people waiting at the property on the allotted day and time. However, you are there for a reason and need to keep your wits about you and take all the necessary notes. You will be greatly aided by doing adequate research, even before you get round to viewing the property.

When you go to a viewing make sure you have the following:

- A tape measure. Check the measurements against those stated in the auction catalogue. You can also use this date for your own plans.
- Camera. This probably goes without saying but you need to get accurate photos of the building, exterior and interior, to act as a record and help you with your own plans.
- A torch. The property may be dark inside and you need to know what you are looking at. Also, a torch may be needed for safety reasons, depending on the condition of the property.
- A note pad or means of taking notes. This is very important as you may need to take copious notes to aid you in making your decision.
- If you can, take a small portable ladder. This should enable you to investigate areas such as loft spaces or cupboards etc.

Using a surveyor

If you are not experienced in carrying out basic property surveys then you might want to employ the services of a surveyor. This might cost, but you will get a firm idea of the structural condition of the property in question. You might want to do several viewings of the property, the first one yourself and then, if needs be, with a surveyor.

The notepad and camera will come in very useful the first time around. You should ensure that you take photos of the external and internal areas of the property. the following are areas that you will want to inspect, and which a surveyor would inspect:

- The envelope of the building. This includes the roof. You should check the roof timbers, tiles, condition of the covering such as the asphalt or felt and if it is a flat roof check for signs of standing water as this indicates that there are problems with the drainage. You might want to look at the eaves of the building, particularly if you wish to convert a loft or install a mansard (roof extension)

- Electrics and plumbing. With the plumbing you need to locate stopcocks and ascertain the condition of the boiler. Check the external guttering and the condition of the soil stack. With the electrics check the age and state of the fuse board which will give you some idea of the state of the wiring. Check wall sockets and check to see if you can see any wiring to ascertain the condition. Look into the loft to see if there are any wires running around. Whilst in the loft look at the existing loft insulation and also look up to see if you can see any daylight, which will indicate roof problems.

- Damp. Check for signs of damp-take photographs so you can ascertain whether it is rising or penetrating damp and just what the extent of work might be.

- Structure of the building. Look closely at the condition of the walls externally or whether there are any signs of movement or cracking and look for evidence of movement around door frames and windows and floor levels.

- Gardens/outside spaces. These areas are quite often ignored by potential bidders. You should look at the condition of gardens, fences and note any boundary lines. To refurbish an outside area takes a lot of time and money and you will want to get this right.

In addition to the above main points, you should make a note of common areas if the property is a flat in a block.

This will indicate the level of expenditure that might be need in the future and how well kept the block is.

You should make a note of any parking arrangements and any pathways that run onto or close to your property. You might also want to have a look to see if the neighbours have carried out any alterations that you could also do to enhance the value of the property, such as an extension.

You may have read the above and decided that checking all of this and arriving at a plan or cost is a tall order. Which is why employing a surveyor might be very necessary. Employing a surveyor might cost about £250 plus VAT for a cursory inspection but it will be well worth it, particularly if you are not an experienced builder or are very experienced in the property game.

As we will see it might cost the same for an inspection of the legal documents but for if you are serious about a property and don't want to end up in trouble further down the line this is money well spent. There are a number of surveys available all with differing costs, as below.

Types of Surveys

The following gives a very brief overview of the different surveys available. When considering the possible purchase of the property the choices are as follows:

- Full Building Survey (most popular survey for most properties).
- Homebuyer Report (previously called a Homebuyer Survey and Valuation).
- Valuation only
- Structural Inspection (General and Specific).
- Home Condition Survey and RICS Condition Survey

Full Building Survey

A full Building Survey on an average house will cost in the order of £300 to £600. It will be carried out by a Chartered Surveyor who is a member of the Royal Institution of Chartered Surveyors (RICS). The Surveyor will normally look at the complete property and give a detailed opinion regarding the state of the building. This is probably now the most popular type of report. It is particularly suitable for older properties or properties which have had major alterations over the years or properties which appear to have problems that need further investigation.

Homebuyer Report or RICS Condition Report

A Homebuyer Report on an average house will cost in the order of £200 to £400. It will be carried out by a Chartered Surveyor who is a member of the Royal Institution of

Chartered Surveyors (RICS) and is licensed to do this work. The Surveyor will normally look at the complete property and give an opinion as to whether the house is value for money to the purchaser. A Homebuyer Report is usually suitable if the house is of modern straight forward construction and has not had any major alterations carried out.

The old 'Homebuyer Survey and Valuation' report used to be very popular until the RICS informed their members that they could no longer carry it out. This has led to a lot of confusion. It should be noted that a lot of Surveyors will carry out a report in the style of the old 'Homebuyer Survey and Valuation' report usually without the valuation. Talking to your chosen Surveyor about the different options is very much recommended.

Valuations

A Valuation only survey on an average house will cost in the order of £250 to £300. It will usually be carried out by a Chartered General Practice Surveyor.

This type of survey is usually done for the benefit of the mortgage lender.

General Structural Inspection

A General Structural Inspection on an average house will cost the in order of £300 to £600. This will normally be performed by a Chartered Engineer who is a member of the Institution of Structural Engineers (IStructE) or the Institution of Civil Engineers (MICE). Some Chartered Surveyors also carry out these inspections. The inspection will concentrate only on the structural aspects of the building (foundations, walls and roof).

It is often useful if the prospective purchaser is intending to carry out a total refurbishment and hence will be replacing the interior decoration and all the services (plumbing, electrics etc).

Specific Structural Inspection

A Specific Structural Inspection is sometimes called for when you have already had some sort of survey and the surveyor has identified a potential structural problem and recommends further investigation.

It should be noted that if a Structural Engineer is requested to look at a specific crack in a building, then he/she will not necessarily look at any other part of the building.

Home Condition Survey and RICS Condition Report

A Home Condition Survey has some similarity to a Homebuyer Report but it does not address the question of value. These are carried out by Home Inspectors with the Dip HI qualification who are members of an accreditation scheme operated either by SAVA or the BRE.

The RICS (Royal Institution of Chartered Surveyors) have also introduced an equivalent survey called a RICS Condition Report which is carried out by licenced Chartered Surveyor. the cost is typically £500.

Other Reports

In some cases, the Surveyor will recommend that further investigations should be considered. In some cases, these would be highly recommended while in other cases they may be just noted and hence bought to your attention. Some of these possible extra investigations could include:

Electrical Report to check the state of the wiring, which if very old could be dangerous.

- Drainage Report to check the drains, which if partly blocked may be causing subsidence.
- Asbestos Report to check for asbestos content and make recommendations.

- Arboricultural Report to make recommendations regarding any trees on the site.

General Tips

It can be useful if the homebuyer can be present while the Surveyor is performing the survey. Some Surveyors are positive towards the idea of meeting the homebuyer at the property but some surveyors are not (understandably the presence of the homebuyer can often be a distraction). A useful compromise that many Surveyors recommend is for the homebuyer to meet the Surveyor at the property towards the end of his inspection. The Surveyor can then point out any particular observations on the spot, in advance of the production of the report. The homebuyer may also have questions along the lines of what are the possible costs for any remedial work that may be required etc.

If you are not able to meet the Surveyor at the site then of course the next best alternative would be to speak to the Surveyor on the telephone as soon as possible after the Survey. It should be remembered that Surveyors can survey a large number of houses in a week and it is not realistic to expect the Surveyor to give an off the cuff verbal report weeks later.

Before placing an order with a Surveyor, you should always ask them to confirm that they have adequate qualifications, accreditation, experience and insurance to perform the work.

Obviously, underpinning your research is what exactly you want the property for, what is its purpose? Are you buying a property to live in, or to eventually sell for a profit or rent?

You will need to do the sums to make sure that what you see is worth investing in and can be a viable rental proposition or there will be a profit when you sell. There are other areas of research for you to do when deciding this.

Using Google maps

I mention Google maps because it is now the most effective tool you can use to carry out fundamental research into a property and its location. Of course, you might have an intimate knowledge of an area and will not need to use this tool. If you don't have this knowledge, you will want to find out where the property is in relation to transport links, industrial areas, schools, shops and other amenities which makes the property an attractive proposition and adds value.

If you don't live in an area then Google maps Streetview function will enable you to walk along a street and see the area in more detail.

Are there any houses which look derelict or might put prospective tenants or purchaser off, or would you want to live there yourself? If you are looking at a commercial property, what kind of an area is it in, what catchment area does it serve?

The legal side of things

When a person buys a property through the conventional route, i.e. through an estate agent, each party to the transaction will have solicitors representing them. A good deal of time will be spent establishing the provenance of the property and establishing whether it is a sound purchase.

In an auction, as we have seen, when you bid for a property, you will only have a maximum of 28 days to complete. Everything must be in place within this time frame. It is vital that you do all of your groundwork before the auction.

Most auction houses will allow prospective purchasers to download legal documents from their sites. This is known as the legal pack. You can do initial checks yourself, and if you feel that you need a solicitor to carry out further checks you can do so. the checks that you can do yourself consist of the following:

- Check to see that there is an Energy performance Certificate (EPC) with the pack. The EPC will tell you an awful lot about the property, the size, whether it is double glazed, the type of insulation, heating and so on. It will also indicate whether further measure need to be taken to improve the overall energy performance. You can factor any costs arising from this into your overall refurbishment budget.

Title to property. This is most important. Right at the outset you will need to know the tenure of the property in question. Is it leasehold or freehold? Most people assume that houses are freehold and flats are leasehold. this is not always the case and there are areas in the UK with a large proportion of freehold flats, for example. This can have an effect on any resale plans as freehold flats can be notoriously difficult to manage and sell on. The data detailing the tenure of the property will come from the Land Registry. If the property is leasehold, the title documents will detail how long the lease is and what ground rent is payable. The legal information relating to a property is critical as it will indicate whether or not you should continue with the purchase, or the bidding, and what the costs may be when it comes to extending a lease. You can also see if there are any charges registered against a property, i.e. a mortgage lender. If you are unsure of anything it is always best to let a solicitor look at it and advise you. the cost is always worth it.

Check to see how long the seller has actually owned the property. There are cases of people buying property and looking for a fast turnaround, *for one reason or another.* The reasons may be that they have bought something that is problematic and want it off their hands.

Title plan. This is a simple drawing which will indicate boundaries of the property that you are buying. Again, it is best, if you are unsure, to let a solicitor look at this. They usually have an expert eye and can spot things that you won't, such as access and right of way issues, flying freeholds (no mans land) etc.

Service charges. My own background as a property manager has taught me that service charges can be one of the most contentious issues surrounding a property. Stories are legion of landlords charging exorbitant service charges and administration fees. There is also the problems of outstanding debts relating to a property that you have just purchased, or are about to bid for. There will be copies of service charge accounts and previous invoices paid on the property in the last three years (or there should be) plus there should be an estimate of future service charge expenditure. It is vital to see and understand this so you know what you are walking into and what you should budget for in the future. For example, this will have a bearing on what rent you can charge in the future and how payment of service charges can affect your profit margins.

Now read the Main Points from Chapter 4 Overleaf

****

Main points from chapter 4

- There are many property auctions being held all over the UK every day. Where you choose to buy at auction very much depends on what you want to buy, what is the intended use for the property, residential investment, commercial investment or a property for your own home.

- The slow housing market and an increase in repossessions have led to more buyers turning to auction houses. But while you may be able to pick up a discount, there are risks involved.

- An auction catalogue consists of Lots, and they will be numbered in the order at which they will be sold at auction. It is the practice of some auction houses to put the most popular lot at the start of the auction so as to draw bidders in.

- The guide prices for properties at auction will vary, depending on what is for sale and where it is. Market forces will dictate this, as they do for property sold in the conventional way. However, for a good many properties the price will be set low, which reflects the condition of the property and also reflects the fact that the auctioneer wants to draw people in to bidding.

- Viewing times are usually set by the auction and shown in their catalogue and you will have to fit in with these time. They are very much like estate agents block bookings. The number of viewings is limited and you will usually get the opportunity to view three or four times before auction. If you are not experienced in carrying out basic property surveys then you might want to employ the services of a surveyor. This might cost, but you will get a firm idea of the structural condition of the property in question. You might want to do several viewings of the property, the first one yourself and then, if needs be, with a surveyor.

- Most auction houses will allow prospective purchasers to download legal documents from their sites. This is known as the legal pack. You can do initial checks yourself, and if you feel that you need a solicitor to carry out further checks you can do so.

****

Chapter 5

Obtaining Finance for an Auction Property

Financing an auction property

Property auctions have the main advantage that generally prices are lower (sometimes up to 50% lower) than high street estate agents. Also, the auction process is quick and produces an instant sale. You know you have bought the property once the hammer falls. No making offers and waiting for a response or being gazumped at the 11th hour.

As we have discussed, properties that you would not see in the high street estate agents find their way into auctions: distressed sales and "fire sales", repossessions, run-down and derelict properties, and often properties at auction that are in need of some repairs or refurbishment. You are dealing in the trade or "wholesale" market here and you need to be prepared to roll your sleeves up and get your hands dirty! But there's lots of opportunity to get a bargain and then add value.

Buying at auction can be a riskier process: you really do need to know what you are doing, to have done your homework (due diligence) and to have your finance arranged beforehand.

Paying cash

Paying cash on the day is the ultimate way of buying an auction property. This gives you greater flexibility and more freedom and is cheaper as you are not paying any fees or interest and are not encumbered by the rules of lending organisations. However, not that many individuals have large quantities of cash to play with and therefore resort to borrowing the costs of purchase.

Borrowing money to fund a purchase

Once you spot the property you are interested in, you need to act fast as there will be a limited amount of time in which to do your due diligence research and arrange your finance before the auction takes place. Property auction finance is normally based on the market value of the property, not the purchase price, which means if you spot a real bargain it is possible to achieve 100% funding on the purchase. It's vital that you are aware that normally you must pay a 10% deposit on the day of the auction. You have then committed yourself to going through with the total purchase within the timescale set - usually 28 days. Finance can be arranged for residential and commercial property auction purchases. The type of finance that you need will depend upon the condition of the property you intend to buy and its subsequent use.

You will need to discuss your purchase plans with an advisor to agree a finance plan of action to ensure that the right auction funding is put in place in time. This process will involve the preparation of a surveyor's valuation report.

Buy-to-Let Mortgages may be one solution and can sometimes be arranged within the timescale, but this may not always be the best solution.

Development or Refurbishment Finance is one answer when you need some minor or major work to the property. You may need property development finance in this situation. 100% financing can be arranged for viable schemes.

Bridging Finance is usually the preferred solution for auction purchases because of the timescale involved. This type of finance is quite appropriate for auction purchases and is not necessarily expensive. There are some very competitive deals available if you know where to source them.

Commercial mortgages and finance can be arranged for limited companies and for private individuals with good credit histories.

Even those with problem credit histories, county court judgments (CCJ's), arrears or IVA's can be accommodated. One such website for property auction finance is https://www.target-mortgages.co.uk.

Property auction purchases have become more popular as demand for property and property investment has increase over the last 15 years or so. The number of properties sold at auction since 1999 has risen by around 70%-around 20,000 residential homes are now sold through UK auctions each year. This has undoubtedly had an effect on prices and in some cases properties at auction have been fetching almost prices you would expect to pay in the high street.

All the more reasons to use caution when buying at auction: calculate exactly what the property is worth to you and don't pay more.

What you should do:

- Do your estimates: building work, refurbishment and fitting out, letting costs, financing costs, legal and professional fees, plans drawing, planning and change of use costs, valuation costs. Know exactly what the project is likely to cost you then add 10% for contingencies.

- Calculate your expected returns on the investment project and know exactly what the property is worth to you as an investment - don't get carried away and pay more.

Now read the main points from Chapter 5 overleaf.

****

Main points from Chapter 5

- Paying cash on the day is the ultimate way of buying an auction property. This gives you greater flexibility and more freedom and is cheaper as you are not paying and fees or interest and are not encumbered by the rules of lending organisations.

- However, not that many individuals have large quantities of cash to play with and therefore resort to borrowing the costs of purchase.

- Once you spot the property or properties you are interested in, you need to act fast as there will be a limited amount of time in which to do your due diligence research and arrange your finance before the auction takes place.

- Property Auction Finance is normally based on the market value of the property, not the purchase price, which means if you spot a real bargain, it is possible to achieve 100% funding on the purchase.

- It's vital that you are aware that normally you must pay a 10% deposit on the day of the auction. You have then committed yourself to going through with the total purchase within the timescale set - usually 28 days.

- Finance can be arranged for residential and commercial property auction purchases. The type of finance that you need will depend upon the condition of the property you intend to buy and its subsequent use.

****

Chapter 6

Doing Your Sums-What to Bid for a Property

What you intend to bid for a property will be the end result of what you have planned to do with it. If you are looking for an investment with a potential return then it is vitally important that you have a handle on all the costs involved, the costs of purchase (often overlooked) and the bid price plus any other costs of renovation.

The first thing to note is that not all properties will be financially viable. The actual cost of the property and the ultimate refurbishment costs might eliminate any profit. Unless of course you are bidding for a property that you intend to renovate and live in and are not bothered about value in the short term. The next thing to consider when you have spotted a property is the costs of buying. There are a number of hidden costs to pay on top of the actual purchase price and any costs of renovation. The costs are as follows:

Stamp duty

In most cases, the solicitor acting for a purchaser will handle stamp duty returns regarding a property purchase. However, given the relative complexity of the rules around stamp duty it is important that would be purchasers are aware of the costs associated with the purchase of different types of property, although in the cases of purchases at auction, some of the information will not be relevant. The below is a summary of stamp duty land tax.

Rates up to 31st March 2025

Property or lease premium or transfer value

Up to £250,000	Zero
The next £675,000 (the portion from £250,001 to £925,000	5%
The next £575,000 (the portion from £925,001 to £1.5m	10%
the remaining amount (the portion above £1.5m)	12%

Rates from 1 April 2025

Property or lease premium or transfer value

Up to £125,000	Zero
The next £125,000 (the portion from £125,001 to £250,000	2%
The next £675,000 (the portion from £250,001 to £925,000	5%
The next £575,000)the portion from £925,001 to £1.5m	10%
The remaining amount (the portion above £1.5m	12%

If you're buying your first home

You can claim a discount (relief) if the property you buy is your first home:

Up to 31st March 2025.

- no SDLT up to £425,000
- 5% SDLT on the portion from £425,001 to £625,000

If the price is over £625,000, you follow the rules for people who've bought a home before.

Discount from 1 April 2025

You'll pay:

- no SDLT up to £300,000
- 5% SDLT on the portion from £300,001 to £500,000

If the price is over £500,000, you cannot claim the relief. Follow the rules for people who've bought a home before.

New leasehold sales and transfers

When you buy a new residential leasehold property you pay SDLT on the purchase price of the lease (the 'lease premium') using the rates above.

If the total rent over the life of the lease (known as the 'net present value') is more than the SDLT threshold), you'll pay SDLT at 1% on the portion of net present value over:

- £250,000
- £125,000 for purchases from 1 April 2025
- This does not apply to existing ('assigned') leases.

Higher rates for additional properties

You'll usually have to pay 5% on top of SDLT rates if buying a new residential property means you'll own more than one.

If you're replacing your main residence

You will not pay the extra 5% SDLT if the property you're buying is replacing your main residence and that has already been sold. If you have not sold your main residence on the day you complete your new purchase you'll have to pay higher rates. This is because you own 2 properties. You can apply for a refund if you sell your previous main home within 36 months. There are special rules if you own property with someone else or already own a property outside England, Wales and Northern Ireland.

Rates if you're not a UK resident

If you're not present in the UK for at least 183 days (6 months) during the 12 months before your purchase you are 'not a UK resident' for the purposes of SDLT. You'll usually pay a 2% surcharge if you're buying a residential property in England or Northern Ireland on or after 1 April 2021.

You may not have to pay a surcharge on certain properties, transactions or if you're a particular type of buyer. Check the rules on who has to pay the surcharge, when you do not have to pay, and if you can claim relief. If you have to pay the surcharge, you'll also have to pay any other rates of SDLT that apply, for example:

- if you already own a property and you're buying an additional property
- if you're a first-time buyer

Special rates

There are different SDLT rules and rate calculations for:

- corporate bodies
- people buying 6 or more residential properties in one transaction
- shared ownership properties
- multiple purchases or transfers between the same buyer and seller ('linked purchases')
- purchases that mean you own more than one property
- companies and trusts buying residential property

Rates for non-residential and mixed land and property

You pay SDLT on increasing portions of the property price (or 'consideration') when you pay £150,000 or more for non-residential or mixed (also known as 'mixed use') land or property. You must still send an SDLT return for most transactions under £150,000. Non-residential property includes:

- commercial property, for example shops or offices
- property that isn't suitable to be lived in
- forests
- agricultural land that's part of a working farm or used for agricultural reasons
- any other land or property that is not part of a dwelling's garden or grounds
- 6 or more residential properties bought in a single transaction
- You pay residential SDLT rates on agricultural land if it's sold as part of the garden or grounds of a dwelling, for example a cottage with fields.
- A 'mixed' property is one that has both residential and non-residential elements, for example a flat connected to a shop, doctor's surgery or office.

Freehold sales and transfers

Property or lease premium or transfer value

Up to £150,000	Zero
the next £100,000 (the portion from £150,001 to £250,000)	2%
the remaining amount (the portion above £250,000)	5%

New leasehold sales and transfers

When you buy a new non-residential or mixed leasehold you pay SDLT on both the:

- purchase price of the lease (the 'lease premium') using the rates above
- value of the annual rent you pay (the 'net present value')

These are calculated separately then added together. If you buy an existing ('assigned') lease, you only pay SDLT on the lease price (or 'consideration'). The net present value (NPV) is based on the total rent over the life of the lease. You do not pay SDLT on the rent if the NPV is less than £150,000.

Net present value of rent

£0 to £150,000	Zero
The portion from £150,001 to £5,000,000	1%
The portion above £5,000,000	2%

Land and property transfers

You may have to pay Stamp Duty Land Tax (SDLT) if the ownership of land or property is transferred to you in exchange for any payment (or 'consideration'). The rules around SDLT depend on the specific circumstances surrounding the transfer. You may be eligible for Stamp Duty Land Tax (SDLT) reliefs if you're buying your first home and in certain other situations. HM Revenue and Customs (HMRC) has guidance on SDLT reliefs.

For full details of SDLT on all property transactions go to: www.gov.uk/stamp-duty-land-tax/land-and-property-transfers.

Other costs-Legal costs

Sometimes with auction properties, one reason why they are being sold at auction is that there is a sticky legal problem to be resolved. There may be a need to extend the lease or sort out rights of way, whatever, it all adds up!

Costs of raising finance to purchase the property. As we know, there are costs to raising finance, such as administration costs, arrangement fees and several other ancillary costs that you need to be fully aware of.

Building survey-we have discussed the costs of the various types of survey-you need to decide whether you need a survey, what kind and factor this cost in.

Property insurance-when you buy property at an auction you will need to insure it from the day of exchange. If the property is empty then a higher premium for non-occupation will apply. You will need to ensure that all details, such as works to the property are communicated to the insurer. It is worth looking to see if the property, if leasehold, benefits from insurance under the freeholder's policy.

How to determine what price to pay at the auction

As we have discussed, there are several motives for buying property at auction-personal dwelling or investment are two of the main motives. The starting point for any bid will be knowledge of the current value of the property as it stands at auction and the end value of the property once all the works are complete. The bit in the middle, the most important bit, is what are the costs of restoring the property to a good condition?

If the cost of the property plus the refurbishment costs are less than the value of the property in good condition then you have made, or can make, a profit. If you intend to rent out the property then you will want a healthy return on capital, which can be measured against the overall cost. What you need to do is to understand the market local to the property that is being sold. You need to do your research and get to know comparable prices in the area. There are plenty of estate agents and the old method of foot slogging around them all will enable you to see the prices in an area. Alternatively, you can do this from the comfort of your armchair by searching the web. The below represents a list of websites that can assist you in your research.

Rightmove-www.rightmove.co.uk. This is the biggest of them all and they have property for sale all over the UK. they have a number of useful tools such as a price comparison report, where you can see sold prices.

Zoopla-www.zoopla.co.uk likewise a leading site which is similar to Rightmove and also enables you to obtain comparisons.

Nethouseprices www.nethouseprices.com this site lists all the actual sold prices in the UK.

Property Price Advice www.propertypriceadvice.co.uk this site provides a basic online valuation of a property.

There are of course more sites which are roughly similar but the above will prove useful to your research. There are also sites which can provide average property prices and market trends for different areas. These are useful if you are trying to track increases (or falls) in property prices. The House Price Index, which is based upon data from the Land Registry can be useful. www.landregistry.gov.uk.

The Registers of Scotland, which is the Scottish equivalent of the Land Registry provides a similar service. See www.ros.gov.uk.

The Halifax and Nationwide also have price indexes. See www/lloydsbankinggroup.com/media1/economic_insight/ halifax_house_price_index_page.asp and www.nationwide.co.uk/hpi/defauklt.htm.

The more that you know about property prices and trends the better equipped you will be to understand exactly what you can bid for a property to make it viable.

In the final chapter of this book, I will be using a day at an auction to highlight all the factors involved in the purchase of several residential properties and one commercial property. This includes calculations of all costs of purchase and renovation and likely profits.

Knowledge of the local area

Of course, if you are born and bred in the area where you intend to purchase property you will probably know and understand all the finer points of what to buy and where to buy, what can be rented out and so on. However, you may not know an area and need to undertake some research to gain knowledge. There are a number of sites which can assist you in this research.

UKLocalArea will enable you to get an idea of the profile of a neighbourhood. You type in a postcode and get back an immediate profile which includes schools, railway stations and other data such as local school performance. www.uklocalarea.com.

If you require more detailed statistics relating to an area, right down to birth and death rates go to www.neighbourhoodstatistics.gov.uk. For crime in an area see www.police.uk. For more details on specific schools you should visit the Ofsted website: https://www.gov.uk/government/organisations/ofsted.

There are other factors you may want to consider, such as the nature of the local environment which can be obtained from the Environment Agency: www.environment-agency.gov.uk.

Calculating the cost of works to a property

Having looked at property research it is now time to get down to the nitty-gritty of calculating what works might be needed to bring a property up to standard. Only when you have done these sums can you know what it is worth bidding for a property. Again, in the final chapter there will be examples laid out.

If you have a builder friend or relative then this will save a lot of time and trouble. You can look at the property with them and arrive at a back-of-an-envelope calculation. Most builders usually know what they are talking about. However, if you are carrying out the initial survey yourself you will need to plan the works, i.e. know what you want and the property needs, for example if it is completely run down then new bathroom, kitchen, rewire, re-plastering, re-plumbing and so on, and then get a quote from an independent builder.

Lists of reputable builders can be obtained from your local authority or by visiting www.checkatrade.com. This site enables you to get in touch with builders who have passed their assessment and are recommended by them.

The best thing to do is to take a builder on site with you and give you an estimate then and there. Their estimate will not be exact and will not be binding but will enable you to see what kind of work is required. Other things to consider are what you want to get out of the building-do you want to sell for a profit and if so what standard of finish do you want? Do you want to rent it out and if so what standard of finish will you want? Do you want to live in it yourself, in which case you may want to arrive at a completely different standard of finish.

Selling costs

If you intend to sell a property after you have renovated it you will need to deduct the selling costs from your final profit. Selling costs can be quite hefty and can erode your profits quite heavily, particularly estate agents' fees. It is often cheaper to use online agents although if you do you will need to arrange and undertake viewings yourself. When you watch programmes such as Homes Under the Hammer, the actual auction costs and other costs are never really highlighted. It is very important that you have a handle on all the costs involved.

Calculating the bid price of a property

After you have undertaken all of your research and know what the build and on-costs are, you should be in a position to know what you can bid for a property, what is your ceiling price. You will want to prepare a calculation that will aid you in this process, which is a simple list, as follows:

- The market value of the property in its current state (£60,000) with discount applied this is £54,000.
- The costs involved in buying (£3,800)
- The costs of works to restore the property (£15,000)
- Auction discount £6,000
- Value of property when finished £95,000

(The auction discount is the reduction in price of the property when placed in the auction, typically 10%).

As you can see from this example, the initial bid price is £54,000. If you got the property for this (most bidding will start under this price) then your costs overall will be £78,800 to bring it up to market value of £95,000. Therefore, there is a potential profit of £16,200 to be made. This will diminish as the bidding gets higher, if it gets higher, so you will need to arrive at a point at which you will not go above.

In this case, if £10,000 profit is your minimum then you wouldn't want to go above around £60,000. By doing your sums this way, you will arrive at a fairly accurate figure which will inform your bidding. As far as costs go, it is always better to allow a bit more than you have anticipated as there will always be those problems that arise that you didn't foresee.

Rental yields and capital yields

The above represents the sale price of a property and the potential profit. However, you might be investing for a different reason, i.e. to rent out. You will also want to know what the capital appreciation is after all works.

Investment properties that are rented out receive an income from tenants. In order to calculate the gross rental yield the annual rental income is divided by the purchase price of the property (annual rent÷price) X 100 = Gross rental yield).

So, if the property was purchased for £75,000 (total) and the rent received is £450 per month the yield would be: £5400 (annual rent) ÷ £75,000 X 100 which equals an annual yield of 7.2. This is a very respectable return on your capital.

Of course, if you are a landlord then you will want to factor in the costs of being a landlord, such as maintenance, insurance, loan costs, empty periods etc.

Capital yields

If and when a property increases in value with time, this is known as capital growth. A simple example is if you buy a property for £75,000 and it increases by 25% there will be a capital appreciation of £18,750. It is a rule of thumb that low price properties might produce a high rental yield and low capital growth and vice-versa, although this is not always the case.

Buying property before auction

It is, of course, possible to purchase a property before it actually goes to auction. All the conditions of sale in the auction room apply, the only difference being is that the property will be withdrawn from auction.

When buying before auction, you will need to find out from the auctioneer whether or not the buyer will accept a price before sale. If so, you will then have to agree a price with the seller.

The price will have to be attractive enough to persuade the seller to sell before auction. therefore, you will need to work out a price that is likely to be accepted.

Again, using all the knowledge that you have gained from this chapter you should probably go towards your ceiling and make the offer. You will still, in most cases, be liable for auctioneer's costs

Now read the Main Points from Chapter 6 overleaf.

****

Main points from chapter 6

- What you intend to bid for a property will be the result of what you have planned to do with it. If you are looking for an investment with a potential return then it is vitally important that you have a handle on all the costs involved, the costs of purchase (often overlooked) and the bid price plus any other costs of renovation.

- The first thing to consider when you have spotted a property is the costs of buying. There are a number of hidden costs to pay on top of the actual purchase price and any costs of renovation.

- The starting point for any bid will be knowledge of the current value of the property as it stands at auction and the end value of the property once all the works are complete. The bit in the middle, the most important bit, is what are the costs of restoring the property to a good condition? If the cost of the property plus the refurbishment costs are less than the value of the property in good condition then you have made, or can make, a profit. If you intend to rent out the property then you will want a healthy return on capital, which can be measured against the overall cost.

- You also need to do your research and get to know comparable prices in the area

****

Chapter 7

The Day of the Auction!

As you can see, an awful lot of time and effort goes into research and preparation when looking for suitable properties at auction.

The day of the auction

Having armed yourself with all you need to know about a particular property, it is assumed that you are comfortable with the property you have selected to purchase at auction and the auction day has arrived. Before you set off to the auction, phone the auction house to make sure the auction is still taking place at the published venue and time and that the lot you are interested in has not been withdrawn.

If you are successful in bidding for your lot then you will need to put down a deposit of ten percent. Sometimes if the value of the property is less than twenty thousand pounds then the minimum deposit is two thousand pounds. The deposit cannot be paid for in cash or credit card and you must take along two items for proof of identity such as a passport and utility bill.

Make sure you arrive at the auction at least an hour before the auction starts. This will give you time to register, if necessary, and to check any last-minute special conditions relating to your lot. Some auction houses require you to register, then give you a card with a number on it so that if you are the successful bidder for a lot then you are easily identifiable. Familiarise yourself with the auction room and find a place where you have good vision of all the other bidders so you can get an idea of who is bidding against you.

The role of the auctioneer

In the auction room, the main person is the auctioneer. It is his or her skill in selling the property that dominates. It is the job of the auctioneer to get the highest price that they can for the property, both for the vendor and for their own fee income. Auctioneers will have different styles of conducting sales depending on where the auction house is and the culture of a particular house. Their styles will range from the cajoling to try to get more bids, to the aggressive to try to at least rise above the reserve price.

Notwithstanding their own individual styles, they are all bound by a common code of conduct. The auctioneer will reserve the right to bid on behalf of the vendor. The auctioneer will state this in his or her opening words. What this really means in practice is that, if the bidding has not reached the reserve price, then the auctioneer can take a bid 'off the wall' to try to up the bids to the reserve price. This is known as 'chandelier bidding'.

Bidding for your lot

You will want to be in a position where you can be clearly seen by the auctioneer. If you have a lot in your sights then you will want to ensure that, when the time comes for a bid you can be clearly seen and heard. The best tactic is to arrive as early as possible and to obtain a prominent seat, as close to the front as possible but not right at the front.

When the auction starts the auctioneer will direct you to a copy of the general conditions of sale for the auction but will not actually read them out. You should be familiar with them before the auction. They will briefly explain the bidding process and then the auction will begin. The auctioneer will give a very brief description of the lot and then ask for the bidding to begin. As a rough estimate the auctioneer will process between twenty and twenty-five lots per hour though this may vary.

When the auctioneer announces your lot, it is time for you to go into action. Make sure you bid clearly so that the auctioneer registers your bid. The old myth that if you scratch your nose you have made a bid is not true. Your bid will only be registered if the auctioneer sees a definite gesture. The bidding process is quite organised with the auctioneer only ever registering the bids of two people until one drops out and then they look for another bidder. You may not even get to bid if the current bidders go above your ceiling.

Telephone bids are quite common with someone from the auction house bidding on behalf of the person on the telephone. Quite often the auctioneer will open the bidding with one person making a bid and then no other bids until the auctioneer has announced the property will be sold on the third and final asking.

At this point just as the hammer is about to come down someone makes a bid and the bidding war starts. Keep in mind the ceiling price that you calculated before the auction and stop bidding when the price gets to your limit. Do not get carried away with the emotion of the auction room and start bidding above the limit you set yourself before the auction.

If you are successful in your bid for your desired lot then you may be asked to hold up the card with the number given to you when you registered for the auction and a member of the auction house staff will come to find you.

Bidding in increments

What to bid is quite important. If you think that the property is yours if you bid way above the reserve price too soon then you might find that you have paid too much. Better bidding in increments to keep the rises in check. You can bid late by jumping in at the last moment, taking everyone by surprise and knocking them off balance. In this way you can achieve what you want. My own recent experience suggests that you can gain what you want by bidding late but then bidding in small increments.

There will be some forms to fill in and the deposit to be paid plus a fee to the auction house that is usually up to £750 although this will vary and can be lower or higher.

You should ensure that you have the following on you when you go to auction:

(overleaf)

- Photographic proof of identification. This can be a passport or driving licence
- Proof of residential address with a bill or bank statement dated within the last three months
- Cleared funds, i.e. proof that you can pay your 10% deposit then and there.

The balance of the money will be required to be paid by you within twenty-eight days although sometimes you may have to complete within fourteen days if stipulated by the vendor. Make sure your solicitor is aware that time is of the essence and that you need to complete quickly.

Unsold property at auction

Around three quarters of all property at auction is usually sold. This will depend on the auction and what is for sale. However, If the bids for a property are not accepted because they do not reach a level close enough to the reserve price that has been set for the property then the lot will be withdrawn from the auction (sometimes left to the auctioneer's discretion at the instruction of the seller). If you are still interested in the property then see the auctioneer after the auction. There may be a deal to be done with the vendor. Many buyers will do a deal with the seller after the auction if the property remains unsold. This is known as 'Hawking'. If you buy after auction then auction conditions still apply and time is of the essence. If others are interested in the same property, it is the first person to submit money and exchange contracts who will win.

Withdrawn property

Sometimes and for no apparent reason the property that you are interested in might be withdrawn. This could be that the vendor has sold pre-auction or that there are problems with the estate. If you have spent any money prior to auction on checking the property out, either surveyors' costs or legal costs, then you will lose this as the vendor has no responsibility for any losses incurred.

Now read the main points from chapter 7 overleaf.

****

Main points from chapter 7

- Before you set off to the auction, phone the auction house to make sure the auction is still taking place at the published venue and time and that the lot you are interested in has not been withdrawn.

- If you are successful in bidding for your lot then you will need to put down a deposit of ten percent. Sometimes if the value of the property is less than twenty thousand pounds then the minimum deposit is two thousand pounds. The deposit cannot be paid for in cash or credit card

- In the auction room, the main person is the auctioneer. It is his or her skill in selling the property that dominates. It is the job of the auctioneer to get the highest price that they can for the property, both for the vendor and for their own fee income.

- When the auctioneer announces your lot, it is time for you to go into action. Make sure you bid clearly so that the auctioneer registers your bid. The old myth that if you scratch your nose you have made a bid is not true. Your bid will only be registered if the auctioneer sees a definite gesture.

- What to bid is quite important. If you bid way above the reserve price too soon then you might find that you have paid too much. Better bidding in increments to keep the rises in check.

****

Chapter 8

Procedure After the Auction

For those who have bought their first property at auction, the initial feeling is usually one of elation and success. For the more seasoned, well it's just another day. Whatever, there will be the business to be taken care of.

Exchange of contracts

I have emphasised throughout the book that as soon as the gavel falls the buyer must be in the position to exchange contracts. The moment that a contract is formed is the moment that the auctioneer brings down the gavel. What happens after the auction is that a memorandum will be signed which is a brief contract and constitutes exchange of contracts. Importantly here, the auctioneer has the legal right to sign the contract on behalf of buyer and seller. This is convenient in that if either the buyer or seller cannot be present at the auction the auction house can take care of the business. Once the auction is complete a member of the auction house staff will find you and accompany you to sign contracts.

See overleaf for a sample Memorandum of sale.

SAMPLE AUCTION SALES MEMORANDUM

THE LOT	
THE PRICE (EXCLUDING VAT)	£
DEPOSIT PAID	£
BALANCE PAYABLE	£
NAME AND ADDRESS OF SELLER	
NAME AND ADDRESS OF BUYER	

NAME AND ADDRESS OF BUYERS SOLICITORS	
THE SELLER AGREES TO SELL AND THE BUYER AGREES TO BUY THE LOT FOR THE PRICE. THIS AGREEMENT IS SUBJECT TO THE CONDITIONS SO FAR AS THEY APPLY TO THE LOT. WE ACKNOWLEDGE RECEIPT OF THE DEPOSIT	
SIGNED BY THE SELLER	
DATE	
SIGNED BY US AS AN AGENT FOR THE SELLER DATE	

This memorandum includes the auction lot number, address of lot, price payable and deposit paid. One copy is signed and dated by or on behalf of the buyer and one copy will be signed by or on behalf of the vendor. The two documents are then exchanged. Bingo! Exchange of contracts. There is no way out from this point. You are legally bound.

It is at the memorandum stage that you provide identification and pay deposit and buyer's premium. It is also the time for you to appoint a solicitor, if one is not already waiting in the wings. You will also need to inform whichever finance company is funding the purchase. Insurance should also be arranged.

If you are delayed or can't complete

Because we don't live in a perfect world, sometimes delays might occur in the purchase of the property. This is usually for finance reasons. The sale contract will lay out penalty's which will have to be paid if the contractual completion date is overrun. If this is going to happen, you should always let your solicitor know so that he or she can sort it out.

If the sale cannot be completed, this is where things can get very complicated. You will lose your deposit for certain.

If the vendor resells the property and the sale proceeds are less than what he would have got from selling to you then the vendor is entitled to take legal action against you to recover the difference between what he has sold it for and the price agreed by you.

There are very few occasions where you can get out of the purchase. It is the full responsibility of the buyer to carry out all checks necessary before bidding for a property. The Property Misdescriptions Act 1991 can apply if the property has been grossly misrepresented but Auction houses usually have everything sewn up regarding this. If you do believe that a property has been misrepresented then you will have to inform your solicitor of this straight away before finally completing the sale.

Now read the main points from Chapter 8 overleaf.

****

Main points from chapter 8

- As the gavel falls the buyer must be in the position to exchange contracts. The moment that a contract is formed is the moment that the auctioneer brings down his gavel. What happens after the auction is that a memorandum will be signed which is a brief contract and constitutes exchange of contracts.

- It is at the memorandum stage that you provide identification and pay the deposit and buyer's premium. It is also the time for you to appoint a solicitor.

- If the sale cannot be completed, this is where things can get very complicated. You will lose your deposit for certain.

****

Chapter 9

A Day at the Auction

We attended an auction held by Graham Penny at Nottingham Racecourse several years ago, commencing at 11.30am. There were approximately 40 lots on offer in the catalogue although 4 had been withdrawn on the day.

We registered for the auction and gave all details and showed proof of identity. We also had to provide proof that we had solicitors instructed before we could bid. In case we didn't have solicitors there were several firms offering their services. There were also other firms in attendance offering finance and building services.

The auction was well attended, with about 140 people occupying a room holding 100 seated. There were several telephone bidders to the left of the room. The auction was being filmed for 'Homes Under the Hammer' to be aired sometime in the future.

Bidding for lots

My business partner and I found two properties in the auction catalogue that we were interested in bidding for a three bed semi detached property in a fairly poor state of repair with a guide price of £68,000 and a two/three bed structurally detached property in (very) poor state of repair for £45,000.

Three bed semi-detached

This property would be ideal for rental purposes and, although it needed approximately £6,000 spent on it would seem to offer both capital growth and an average rental yield. We used various sites, mentioned in the previous chapter, to ascertain that the neighbourhood is sound and free from crime, there were good local amenities such as transport and schools and there were no adverse works planned which could affect the price of the property. Therefore, we decided that the property would be a good investment for sale or rent.

As I am a property manager, we dispensed with the services of a surveyor and carried out our own cursory survey on the viewing day. Although there were people swarming over the property we still managed to come up with a credible plan. We judged that the following needed to be done to the property to bring it back up to a high standard, in keeping with the rest of the properties in the street:

NEW KITCHEN

NEW BATHROOM AND SHOWER

NEW BOILER

SOME REPAIR WORK FROM INGRESS OF DAMP FROM THE ROOF

MINOR REPAIRS TO THE ROOF

FULL DECORATION THROUGHOUT

GARDEN TIDYING UP AT REAR
FULL REWIRE

TOTAL £6,000

Research on Rightmove showed that a similar property in the same street sold for £115,000. We believed we could achieve £120,000.

In terms of capital growth and profit from instant sale, the following were our calculations:

Cost of property at auction £96,000 against £68,000 guide price.
Legal costs £950 plus VAT (£1240)
2.5% auction fee £750plus VAT = £900
TOTAL £98,140
Costs of refurbishment
£6,000
Total £104,140
Costs of sale
Priced at £125,00 to achieve £120,00
Estate agents' fees 2% Say sale at £120,000 = £2400 plus VAT = £2880
Legal fees £1200 including VAT

No finance fees as we would pay with cash. However, it is important if you are using borrowed money to factor the costs of finance in.

Total £4080

Total sale profit

Costs of purchase and refurbishment £104,140

Sale price £120,000

Costs of sale £4080

Potential Profit £11,780

Therefore, the property would achieve a healthy profit. Don't forget to factor in any other costs such as buildings insurance. Let's look at the rental yields available.

Rental yields

Research on Rightmove and Zoopla revealed that the rental returns on this type of property would be around £500-550 per calendar month.

The following costs would be associated with rental:

Buildings Insurance £200 per year

Initial costs of furnishing property (white goods) £750

Annual gas and electric checks £300

Costs of agency if using agency to find tenant (initial £500 plus VAT)

There would be a monthly management fee of around 10% to factor in if using an agent to manage the property. In this case there are no mortgage costs as we would pay cash, however, in many cases there is a monthly mortgage payment to consider.

Rental yield

As we have seen the rental yield is calculated by annual rental (£6000) divided by the price (£104,140) times 100 = annual yield 5.76 per annum.

Given that we are using our own cash there are no hefty financing costs so the overall yield is very reasonable. However, taxation should be considered. It is very necessary to employ an accountant who is knowledgeable about the in's and out's of buy-to-let property accounting.

Lot 2. Overleaf.

Structurally detached two/three bed property.

This property did not sell at the guide price of £45,000 and was eventually withdrawn. However, we have calculated a potential return below as if it had sold at £60,000. We carried out the same checks as before regarding neighbourhood and general area, which revealed that the property was in a very desirable area. However, the low price reflected the very run-down state of the property. 'Structurally detached' means that, although the property abuts the adjacent house it is in fact detached from it. As before, we dispensed with the services of a surveyor and carried out our own cursory survey. We judged that the following needed to be done to the property to bring it back up to a high standard.

NEW KITCHEN

NEW BATHROOM AND SHOWER

NEW BOILER NEW RADIATORS

NEW ROOF (WELSH SLATE)-New rainwater goods

FULL DECORATION THROUGHOUT

GARDEN SIGNIFICANT WORK AT REAR (garden 150 feet by 50 feet) DEMOLITION OF OUTBUILDINGS

FULL REWIRE

NEW WINDOWS AND DOORS

In addition to the usual works, we judged that this property, which was extremely spacious, could be remodelled to achieve a smaller bathroom and a sizeable third bedroom. This could be achieved by demolishing a chimney breast and reducing the size of the bathroom.

The photo overleaf indicates the size (and condition) of the bathroom.

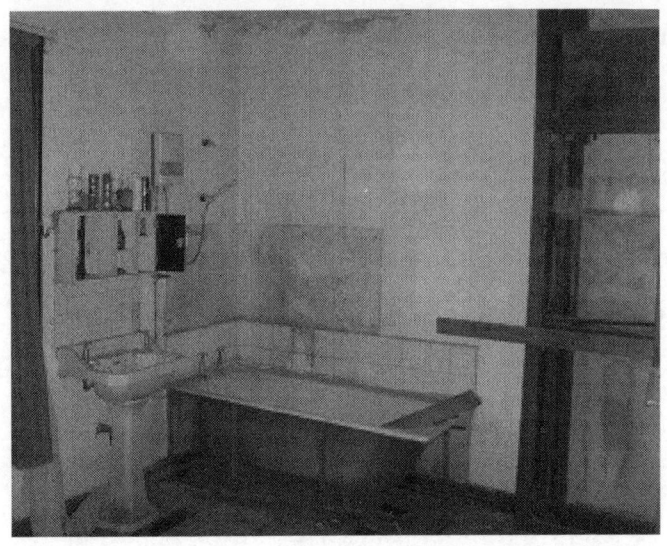

The above bathroom is 10 feet 10 inches by 12 feet 10 inches and could easily be converted into a bedroom by moving a wall to the side (bedroom) reducing both bathroom and bedroom to create a third bedroom. This could be achieved without drastically reducing the overall layout.

An extension could be built at the rear to enhance the ground floor, although this hasn't been factored into the costing. It would be necessary to obtain alternative valuations with the property extended to see if it is worth going down that route.

TOTAL £38,000 with a £5000 contingency for cost overruns.

Although this was an unusual property, and very spacious by normal standards, research on Rightmove showed that a similar property in the same area sold recently for £120,000. Given the unusual nature and location of this property and the size of the garden, we were certain that we could obtain around £125,000.

In terms of capital growth and profit from instant sale, the following were our calculations:

Cost of property at auction £60,000 (final sale cost)

Legal costs £950 plus VAT (£1240)

2.5% auction fee £750plus VAT = £900

TOTAL £62,140

Costs of refurbishment

£43,000 (including contingency costs)

Total £105,000

Costs of sale

Priced at £130,000 to achieve £125,00

Estate agents' fees 2% Say sale at £125,000 = £2500 plus VAT = £3000

Legal fees £1200 including VAT =£1440

No finance fees as we would pay with cash. However, it is important if you are using borrowed money to factor the costs of finance in.

Total £4,440

Total sale profit

Costs of purchase and refurbishment £103,000

Sale price £125,000

Costs of sale £4,440

Potential Profit

£20,560

Therefore, the property would achieve a very healthy profit indeed. Don't forget to factor in any other costs such as buildings insurance.

Rental yields

Research on Rightmove and Zoopla revealed that the rental returns on this type of property would be around £700-750 per calendar month. As this is a one-off property, unusual in its nature, very attractive with a huge garden, we thought that a higher than average rental for the area could be obtained.

The following costs would be associated with rental:

Buildings Insurance £300 per year

Initial costs of furnishing property (white goods) £750

Annual gas and electric checks £300

Costs of agency if using agency to find tenant (initial £750 plus VAT)

There would be a monthly management fee of around 10% to factor in if using an agent to manage the property.

In this case there are no mortgage costs as we would pay cash, however, in many cases there is a monthly mortgage payment to consider.

Rental yield

As we have seen the rental yield is calculated by annual rental (say £725 = £8700) divided by the price (£103,000) times 100 = annual yield 8.44 per annum.

Given that we are using our own cash there are no hefty financing costs so the overall yield is very reasonable. However, taxation should be considered. As we stated above, it is very necessary to employ an accountant who is knowledgeable about the in's and out's of buy-to-let property accounting.

The companion volume to this book, A Straightforward Guide to Letting Property for Profit goes into letting property and taxation issues in more depth.

As a footnote, although we bid for both of the properties, we didn't buy either as the bidding exceeded our ceiling in the case of the first property and the second was withdrawn. However, our calculations made both an attractive investment for us.

****

Conclusion

As you might have gathered by reading this book, although actually buying a property at auction is really just a case of bidding for it, actually knowing what property to buy and what to bid, and what is your ceiling price is the end result of careful research.

You need to know everything about the property and the area that it is in. True, people bid blindly at auction but even they have some idea of what they are buying.

Essentially, you need to look for properties that are sold at an undervalue, you need to know what the refurbishment costs are and what the costs of purchase and sale are (if you intend to sell). If you intend to rent you need to know what the potential rental yield is after costs.

To make a successful bid at auction and then go on to make a profit or gain a decent rental income and capital growth requires prior knowledge of what you are buying and what the area is like, indeed what the town or city is like and what kind of tenants or buyers can be attracted.

Like many things in life, experience counts for a lot in the property auction world. You need to understand the source of finance, building costs and something about building defects. Given that you are making a big investment you need to get it right.

I hope that this brief book has given you an insight into the world of property auctions and an idea of what you need to do, and what background work is required when purchasing a property at auction.

Good luck with you auction experience!

Roger Sproston 2025

****

Glossary of Terms

Actual completion date

The date when completion takes place or is treated as taking place for the purposes of apportionment and calculating interest

Addendum

An amendment or addition to the conditions whether contained in a supplement to the catalogue. This may be a written notice in the catalogue or announced at the auction.

Auction

A public sale in which property or items of merchandise are sold to the highest bidder.

Auctioneer

The person who conducts an auction. The auctioneer introduces each lot offered for sale, acknowledges bids, and announces whether lots are sold or unsold and their final bid prices.

Auction catalogue

The catalogue gives a description of the property, details on how to view each property and the General Conditions of

Sale. These are prepared by the auctioneer, stating the basis on which the auction is carried out.

Bid

The offer to buy property at a specific price.

Completion

On completion of the sale of the lot there is usually a defined period from the auction to the completion date in which the sale must be finalised. Penalties will be applied if the sale is completed late which can include losing your deposit.

Exchanging contracts

If you are the successful bidder at the auction sale, the sale is binding on the fall of the hammer and you will then be asked to sign and exchange contracts in the auction room.

Guide price

A guide price gives an indication of the price that the property is expected to sell for and what the vendor is hoping to achieve. Guide prices are for information only and shouldn't be relied on as an indication of reserve price or representing professional valuations for any purpose.

Purchasers are deemed to have relied on their own knowledge or obtained the independent, professional advice of others.

In the room

A bid from someone in the room (not by phone or the internet.)

Legal pack

The vendor's solicitors prepare a legal pack containing copies of all the legal papers that you and your solicitor are likely to need to make an informed decision about your lot. The pack should include (where applicable) copies of: special conditions of sale, title deeds, leases, office copy entries, searches, replies to pre-contract enquiries. All legal packs will be available for inspection at the auction room. You must be aware that you buy subject to all documentation and terms of contract whether or not you have read them.

Lot

Each separate property described in the catalogue or (as the case may be) the property that the seller has agreed to sell or buy.

Previews or exhibitions

A viewing of the property held in advance of the auction. Pre-auction viewings are open to the public and may be attended at no charge.

Proxy bid

The auctioneers can undertake bidding on behalf of buyers unable to attend the auction in person. The buyers must contact the auction house prior to the auction to obtain an official, proxy bidding form. This must then be returned to the auction house with a deposit cheque within the time specified by the auctioneers.

The buyer writes the maximum amount they will bid to on the form and the auctioneers will bid on behalf of the buyer, up to, but not beyond, the stated price.

Reserve

A reserve price is the lowest price the vendor will accept. This is agreed between the vendor and the Auctioneer. Most properties entered into the auction have a reserve price. This is confidential and not disclosed to any interested parties.

*

Telephone bid

A telephone bid made by a member of staff from the auction house. The staff member telephones the client from the salesroom to bid on particular lots and relays the client's bids to the auctioneer during the bidding on those lots.

Tenancies

Contracts to occupy or lease the property subject to rent. A lot may be sold subject to existing tenancy agreements.

Withdrawal

Failure to reach the reserve price or insufficient bidding. The auctioneer will withdraw the property from the auction.

****

Useful Websites

Trade Magazines

Property Investor News

www.property-investor-news.com/auctions.html.

Auction data and listings

www.auctioniq.co.uk

www.propertyreporter.co.uk

www.propertyweek.com

Bidding by phone
BisX1 (bidding on smart phone)
Bidx1.com

Repossessed Properties
Property data

propertydata.co.uk

Land Auctions

www.ukauctionlist.com

Legal advice

ansons.law/thinking-of-buying-an-auction-property-heres-
what-you-need-to-know

General Organisations

Essential Information Group

https://www.eigpropertyauctions.co.uk

Royal Institute of Chartered Surveyors

www.rics.org

Institution of Structural Engineers (IStructE)

www.istructe.org

Institution of Civil Engineers (MICE)

www.ice.org.uk

Land Registry

www.landregistry.gov.uk

The Registers of Scotland

www.ros.gov.uk

The Environment Agency:

www.environment-agency.gov.uk

Checkatrade

www.checkatrade.com

Property websites

Zoopla

www.zoopla.co.uk

Rightmove

www.rightmove.co.uk

Nethouseprices

www.nethouseprices.com

Property Price Advice

www.propertypriceadvice.co.uk

On the Market

www.onthemarket.com

Property Eye

www.propertyindustryeye.com

General advice

www.unbiased.co.uk

Self-build

www.self-build.co.uk/guide-buying-property-auction

Advice on purchasing property for renovation at auction
https://auction-properties.co.uk/renovation-property-at-auction

****

Index

Mortgage, 40

Planning permission, 19
Probates, 17
Proof of identity, 3, 28
Property Auction News, 47
Property insurance, 92
Property investors, 16
Property Misdescriptions Act 1991, 120
Property surveys, 59
Receivership sales, 17
Rental yields, 6, 99, 127, 133
Repossessions, 15, 17, 50
Residential Investments, 18
Retail shops, 20

Sales particulars, 3, 28
Selling costs, 6, 97
Service charges, 70
Special Conditions of Sale, 21, 39
Specific Structural Inspection, 64
Stamp duty, 6
Structure of the building, 60

Tenanted Properties, 18
Title plan, 70

****

All titles, listed below, in the Straightforward Guides Series, and further books in the Emerald Guides Series, can be purchased online, via Amazon, by going to www.straightfowardbooks.co.uk

Law, Including Emerald Guides

Consumer Rights
Bankruptcy Insolvency and the Law
Employment Law
Healthcare Rights and law
Private Tenants Rights
Family law
Small Claims in the County Court
Contract law
Intellectual Property and the law
Divorce and the law
Leaseholders Rights
The Process of Conveyancing
Knowing Your Rights and Using the Courts
Producing Your own Will
Housing Rights
The Bailiff the law and You
Probate and The Law
Company law

What to Expect When You Go to Court
Give me Your Money-Guide to Effective Debt Collection
Being a Litigant in Person
Conveyancing Residential property
A Practical Guide to Obtaining Probate
Marriage and Same Sex Partnerships
A Guide to Powers of Attorney
Mental Health and the Law

General titles, Including Emerald Guides

Letting Property for Profit
A Straightforward Guide to The Planning System and
Planning permissions
Buying, Selling and Renting property
Bookkeeping and Accounts for Small Business
Creative Writing
Freelance Writing
Writing Your own Life Story
Writing performance Poetry
Writing Romantic Fiction
Speech Writing
The Straightforward Business Plan
The Straightforward C.V.
Successful Public Speaking
Handling Bereavement
Individual and Personal Finance

The Crime Writers casebook
Being a Detective
A Comprehensive Guide to Arrest and Detention
A Comprehensive Guide to Burglary and Robbery
The Bailiff and You
Beating The Bully
Explaining Autism
Explaining Diabetes
Explaining Alzheimer's and Dementia
Explaining Asthma
Stop Smoking Now
Mind Power and Healthy Eating

Go to:

www.straightforwardbooks.co.uk